Is it a Monster?

Written by Joe Elliot

Illustrated by Neil Sutherland, Blue-Zoo and Tony Trimmer

H was running.

Stop, H! Look at this!

3

s-t-**air**-s, stairs!
They all went up the stairs.

I hid under the stairs. The rest went up.

Was a monster waiting at the top? Or a pair of monsters?

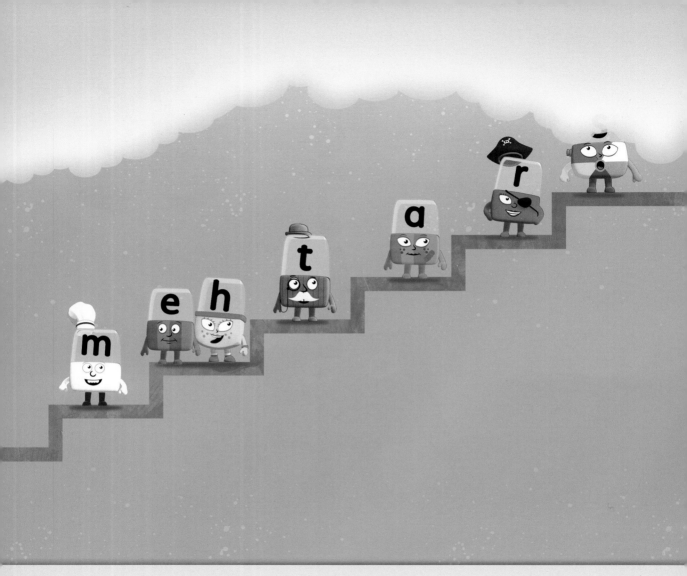

The blocks went high up into the air. Soon they got to the top.

A silver ladder! Look!

They went up the ladder.

They got to a big silver thing.

Rrrr! It is a thing for running in.

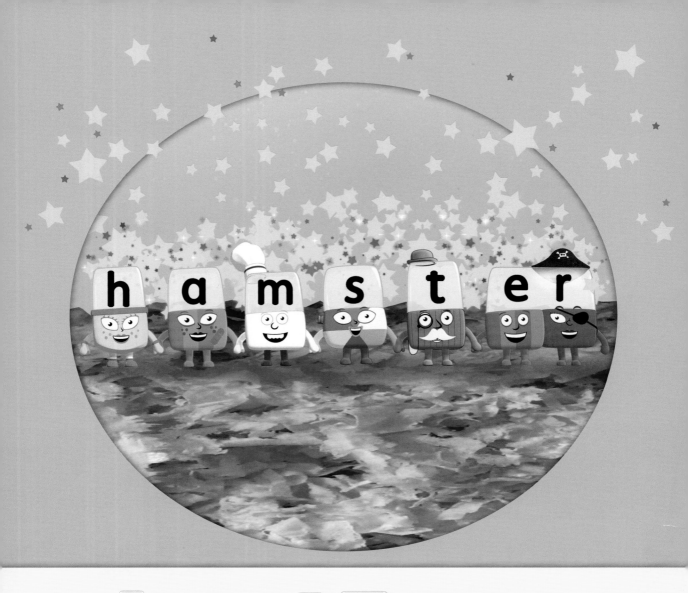

h-a-m-s-t-er, hamster!

The hamster was a
good runner.

They all began to go
back down.

I was still afraid.